Water of Bapti
Water for L

An Activity Book

Anne E. Kitch

Illustrations by Shelley Dieterichs

Morehouse Publishing
NEW YORK · HARRISBURG · DENVER

Morehouse Publishing, 4775 Linglestown Road, Harrisburg, PA 17112

Morehouse Publishing, 445 5th Avenue, New York, NY 10016

Morehouse Publishing is an imprint of Church Publishing Incorporated.
www.churchpublishing.org

Cover design by Laurie Klein Westhafer

Library of Congress cataloging-in-Publication Data

Acknowledgements:

I am pleased to acknowledge Sharon Ely Pearson who conceived of this project and was its enthusiastic champion all along the way. I wish to thank Suzanne Guthrie and Maura Sullivan who read the work in progress offering wisdom and encouragement. I am grateful to my spouse Jim Peck and our daughters Sophie and Lucy, who offered inspiration and acumen as consultants and cheerleaders. AEK

ISBN: 978-0-8192-2782-9

Printed in the United States of America

10 9 8 7 6 45 4 3 2 1

Table of Contents

Water of Baptism, Water for Life

Water is perhaps the essential component of human health, nourishment, security, economic growth, international and regional political stability and environmental sustainability. Water is simultaneously ordinary and extraordinary. Even to spend one day taking into account all the water in our life is an awakening to its power. What water surrounds you at this very moment? Do you notice the humidity in the air, the tears in your eyes, saliva in your mouth, mucus in your nose, moisture in your skin? What water is in your surrounding environment at this moment? A nearby stream or pond? Rain or snow or dewdrops? How far are you at this moment from a sink, toilet, or shower? How easily could you get a drink of cold water?

Jesus said, "whoever gives even a cup of cold water to one of these little ones in the name of a disciple—truly I tell you, none of these will lose their reward." (Matthew 10:42) How wonderful it is to have a cold drink of water on a hot day! But many children in the world do not have clean and safe water to drink. As abundant as water is, not everyone has access to this life-giving resource. Providing clean water for all God's children is an act of justice, love, and respect. Caring for others in this way expresses a core value of what it means to be a Christian.

Water is also essential for baptism--the foundation of our life in Christ. We understand baptism as a sacrament, as a sacred rite of initiation, as something holy. Water is the visible sign of Holy Baptism. Through our baptism we are immersed into our life in the Church and the imperatives of our Baptismal Covenant, which calls us to serve others in the world. The promises we make in baptism compel us to care for all of God's people—and the water that sustains them.

We cannot separate a theology of baptism from a theology of the stewardship of creation. As we are called to care for one another, we are also called to be good stewards of the world that sustains us. Water is foundational to all life. Water is foundational to our faith. It may seem odd to name something as fluid as water as our foundation. Yet water even pre-exists God's creation of the heavens and the earth.

Not surprisingly, water stories abound in the bible. One of the most sophisticated theological discussions in scripture revolves around water. Jesus meets a Samaritan woman at a well and the two of them engage in an astonishing dialogue. At one point, Jesus offers the woman living water. She replies, "Sir, you have no bucket, and the well is deep. Where do you get that living water?" Jesus tells her that what he has to offer is "a spring of water gushing up to eternal life." (John 4:7-15) Our Christian faith continually calls us to make the connection from the living water that Jesus offers to the water we depend on everyday for life. Like the Samaritan woman, we are invited to honor the gift, and to take action to ensure that everyone has access to this gift.

How to Use this Book

We live in a world where water is becoming a scarce and compromised resource. *Water of Baptism, Water for Life* invites young people and adults alike to consider an ethics of water. The activities in this book encourage the understanding that water is essential for all life—physical and spiritual. The book explains that while water is ubiquitous, not all people have equal access to this necessary resource. Older children, especially those who live a life of privilege with easy access to clean water for drink and play, will draw a connection between the gift of water in their lives and the need of everyone to have access to this gift.

Church and School

Christian Educators and Formation Specialists can use this book in a church or school setting for class projects, group discussions and worship times. The activities can help young people become more aware of the importance of environmental sustainability and our part in it. Significant theological concepts, scripture passages and church teachings are highlighted. This book can also be particularly helpful when preparing older children or youth for baptism.

Activities tap into multiple intelligences and offer a variety of ways to interact with the issue of water sustainability in our world and as a core value of our faith. Engaging with these activities will enable young people to make connections between their faith and daily life. This book encourages Christians of all ages to work for justice in the global community through ministry and mission.

The activities in this book cover many topics including baptism, the Baptismal Covenant, creation, salvation history, world mission, prayer, ministry, sustainability, the Millennium Development Goals, water ethics, conservation and economic justice. The activities easily lend themselves to intergenerational groups and to venues such as Vacation Bible School, summer camp and retreat settings.

Families

This book can be explored at home as young people and adults together learn about water ethics in daily life. Pages include service projects as well as devotions that can include all family members regardless of age. Choosing to lessen your water footprint as a household is a great way to better serve your neighbors near and far.

Parents and Godparents can give this book as a gift for a baptismal anniversary or other occasion offering young people an enjoyable way to continue to live into their baptism. Activities and pages can be used in home celebrations on Earth Day, Baptismal feasts and Easter.

Devotional for Home, Church or School

Individuals, families, youth classes or small groups can use this book for a weekly prayer time, as part of a retreat or as daily devotions for a season such as during Advent, Lent or the Fifty Days of Easter.

Activities could be incorporated into the following short prayer service:

🜄 Create a waterscape: begin with a bowl of water. Add a candle, perhaps using a floating candle in the water. Surround the bowl with symbols of life or baptism such as shells, plants, an icon of the Baptism of Christ.

🜄 Gather as a household or group.

🜄 Light the candle.

🜄 Begin with one of the following invitations
— *Leader:* Mightier than the sound of many waters
— *Response:* is the Lord who dwells on high

or

— *Leader:* We feast upon the abundance of your house, O God
— *Response:* You give us drink from the river of your delights

or

— *Leader:* You visit the earth, O God, and water it abundantly
— *Response:* the river of God is full of water

🜄 Explore the Activity page together

🜄 Close with one of the following prayers (or write your own)

Calm me, Lord, as you stilled the storm.
Still me Lord and keep me from harm.
Let all the tumult within me cease.
Enfold me, Lord, in your peace.
Celtic Prayer

or

Dear God, be good to me;
The sea is so wide and my boat is so small.
Breton Fisherman's Prayer

Creation

In the beginning...

Color by number to find the hidden picture.

1) light blue	2) dark blue	3) purple
4) dark green	5) grey	6) black

...when God created the heavens and the earth, the earth was a formless void and darkness covered the face of the deep, while a wind from God swept over the face of the waters.

(Genesis 1:1-5)

Water is Everywhere

Water is the only substance that can be found in nature in all three states of matter: solid, liquid and gas.

Sort the water into the correct column:

rain drop, cloud, stream, glacier, ocean, steam, snow, iceberg, water vapor, hail

Solid	Liquid	Gas
icicle	dewdrop	mist

How many other examples can you think of?

Water = Life

Without water, there would be no life on earth. Plants and animals need water to survive. Our bodies are made up of almost 70% water. Even before we are born, we are protected by water in the womb.

Water is everywhere around us. In the air we breathe, in the trees that give us shade, and in the foods we eat. Sometimes, water seems so ordinary that we don't even notice it. But water is extraordinary, perhaps our most valuable natural resource. Without enough water, all creation suffers. Without clean water, all creation suffers.

Water is also powerful. Water can dissolve solids, cleanse dirt, and bind substances together. We use water to make electricity, power machines and cook food. Water can be destructive in the form of floods, hurricanes, typhoons and ice storms. People, plants and animals can drown in water. Too little or too much water can be life threatening.

Water is an essential element of life, both biologically and spiritually. We are made of it and born out of it. A primal element that pre-exists earth's creation, water can symbolize both life and death.

Klara Tammany, *Living Water: Baptism as a Way of Life*

The Water Cycle

All water is recycled water. Water is not made new, but rather constantly moves through the water cycle. The glass of water you drink contains water molecules that have existed since the beginning of creation. This water has been through <u>transpiration</u>, <u>evaporation</u>, <u>condensation</u>, <u>precipitation</u>, <u>percolation</u> and <u>infiltration</u> over and over again until it ended up in your glass.

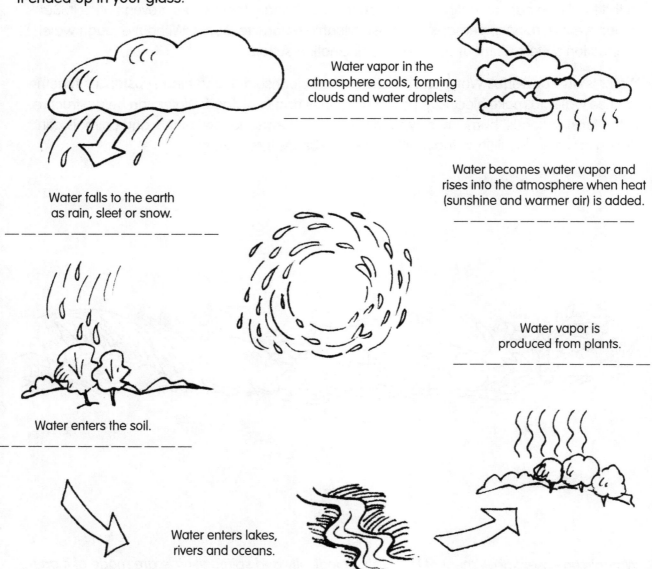

Water vapor in the
atmosphere cools, forming
clouds and water droplets.

_____

Water becomes water vapor and
rises into the atmosphere when heat
(sunshine and warmer air) is added.

_____

Water falls to the earth
as rain, sleet or snow.

_____

Water vapor is
produced from plants.

_____

Water enters the soil.

_____

Water enters lakes,
rivers and oceans.

_____

Use the underlined words to complete the water cycle diagram.

Water Reflection

If you could be any body of water, what would you be? Write or draw about this.

God's Hand in the Water

Even as God began the work of creation, water was already there.

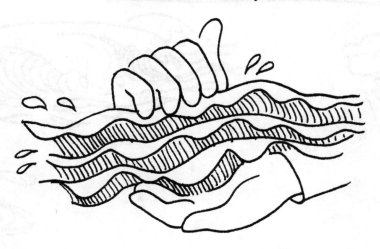

On the first day of creation, God called light into being. On the second and third days of creation, God took hold of the waters. God separated some of the water into the atmosphere. God gathered the remaining water into seas and lakes and rivers, allowing dry land to appear. Then God watered the earth so the land could produce plants and trees. On the fifth day of creation, God called the water to teem with life, creating fish and sea monsters and microbes. (Read Genesis 1:1–2:3)

God called all living things to be fruitful and to multiply: the plants and trees, the fish of the sea, the birds of the air, the animals on land and human beings. Without water, none of God's creation could be fruitful.

As we read the ancient stories of God's people throughout history, we see God's hand in all of life. We see God's hand in water everywhere.

Where do you see the evidence of God's hand in your life? In the world around you?

Safely through the Flood

God brought Noah, his family and the animals safely through the flood in the ark. The waters cleansed the earth and brought forth new life

Find a safe path for the ark through the water.

God said, "This is the sign of the covenant that I make between me and you and every living creature that is with you, for all future generations: I have set my bow in the clouds, and it shall be the sign of the covenant between me and the earth."

(Genesis 9:12-13)

Crossing the Red Sea

Unscramble the words in the story. Then, find the circled letter in each unscrambled word and copy these letters, in order, into the blank spaces at the bottom of the page.

When the Israelites left Egypt, they camped at the edge of the Red Sea hoping they would be safe. But Pharaoh changed his mind about letting them go and began to **sceha** __ __ __ __ (__) them.

The Israelites, believing they were caught between Pharaoh's army and the sea, cried out to God in fear. They became **xemleetry** __ (__) __ __ __ __ __ __ __ angry with Moses and wailed, "why did you bring us out here to be killed?"

God told Moses to lift up his staff and stretch his hands over the sea. Moses did so and God parted the waters so the Israelites **odluc** __ (__) __ __ __ escape.

Pharaoh's army followed the Israelites into the parted waters, but their chariot wheels got **cleodgg** __ __ __ __ __ __ (__) in the mud.

God told Moses to stretch out his hand again. The waters **dutrener** __ __ __ (__) __ __ __ __ to their place, covering the chariots and drowning Pharaoh's army.

But Moses and the Israelites walked on dry ground through the sea, with the **swreat** __ __ __ __ __ (__) forming a wall on their right and on their left.

This story is known as:

The __ __ __ __ __ __

You can read this whole story in the Bible in chapter 14 of the book by the same name.

Water Images

Look up the verses in Psalms to find water words that solve this crossword.*

Across
5. Psalm 93:4
6. Psalm 78:20
8. Psalm 72:6
10. Psalm 77:17
11. Psalm 87:7
13. Psalm 1:3

Down
1. Psalm 133:3
2. Psalm 46:4
3. Psalm 36:9
4. Psalm 65:9
6. Psalm 63:1
7. Psalm 107:35
9. Psalm 56:8
12. Psalm 24:2

*for best results, use the NRSV translation of the Psalms.

The Caring Shepherd

Psalm 23

The Lord is my shepherd;
   I shall not be in want.
He makes me lie down in green pastures
   and leads me beside still waters.
He revives my soul
   and guides me along right pathways for his Name's sake.
Though I walk through the valley of
      the shadow of death,
I shall fear no evil;
   for you are with me;
   your rod and your staff, they comfort me.
You spread a table before me in the presence
      of those who trouble me;
   you have anointed my head with oil,
   and my cup is running over.
Surely your goodness and mercy shall follow me all the
      days of my life,
   and I will dwell in the house of the Lord for ever.

How does God provide water for you? How can you provide water for others? Write or draw about this.

God's Word

For as the rain and snow come down from heaven,
    and do not return there until they have watered the earth,
making it bring forth and sprout,
    giving seed to the sower and bread to the eater, so shall my word
        be that goes forth from my mouth;
    it shall not return to me empty,
but it shall accomplish that which I purpose,
    and succeed in the thing for which I sent it.

                                        (Isaiah 55:10-11)

The prophet Isaiah saw God's Word moving through creation bringing new life over and over again. Draw your own version of the water cycle showing how God's Word brings life.

Baptism = New Life

To initiate means to begin. Baptism is the rite of Christian initiation. That is, a person begins a Christian life by being baptized. Through baptism we are born into God's family, the church. We receive forgiveness of sins and a new life in the Holy Spirit. We understand ourselves to be members of Christ's Body.

A person is baptized with water in the name of the Father, Son and Holy Spirit. Water is the sign of baptism. Whether a person is splashed with water on the forehead or plunged into a lake, through baptism she is immersed in the Holy Spirit. The waters of baptism symbolize death and life. We enter into the waters to die to an old life and to receive a new life.

Once we are baptized, we are always members of the Body of Christ. We say that a person is "marked as Christ's own forever."

John the Baptist

Unscramble the words in the story. Then, find the circled letter in each unscrambled word and copy these letters, in order, into the blank spaces at the bottom of the page to complete the sentence.

John was the son of Elizabeth and Zechariah; he was also a cousin of Jesus. John knew about God's love for humankind and all **crnetioa** __ ◯ __ __ __ __ __ __ .

John also knew that God's people did not always **yeob** __ __ ◯ __ God's laws.

John's ministry was that of a prophet. He **drepaper** __ __ __ ◯ __ __ __ __ the way for the messiah, God's promised savior.

John called **lepope** __ ◯ __ __ __ __ to turn away from sin and to turn back to God.

People came from all over the **croutenisyd** __ __ __ ◯ __ __ __ __ __ __ __ to be baptized by him in the river Jordan, confessing their sins.

John promised them that someone greater than he was coming, who would **ziptabe**

__ __ __ ◯ __ __ __ with the Holy Spirit.

When we __ __ __ __ __ __ __ , we turn away from sin and re-turn to God.

The Baptism of Christ

Jesus came from Nazareth of Galilee and was baptized by John in the Jordan. And just as he was coming up out of the water, he saw the heavens torn apart and the Spirit descending like a dove on him. And a voice came from heaven, "You are my Son, the Beloved; with you I am well pleased." (Mark 1:9-11)

How would you tell this story? Imagine staging it.

As a human tableau that comes to life.

As a film.

As a stop motion animation movie.

How would this story happen in your city or town today? At a fountain? Fire hydrant? Swimming pool? Local river or stream?

Blessing the Water

At the time of Baptism, we thank God for the gift of water and we ask God to bless the water that will bring us new life.

Find the hidden words in the picture to complete this prayer of thanksgiving.

We thank you Almighty God, for the _____ of water. Over it the _____ moved in the beginning of creation. Through it you led the children of Israel out of their bondage in Egypt into the land of _____. In it your Son Jesus received the _____ of John and was anointed by the Holy Spirit as the _____, the Christ, to lead us, through his _____ and resurrection, from bondage of _____ into everlasting life.

We thank you for the_____ of Baptism. In it we are buried with _____ in his death. By it we share in his resurrection. Through it we are _____by the Holy Spirit.

(The Book of Common Prayer, p. 306)

Searching the Waters

Find these baptismal words in the water.

refresh   water   font   blessing   life   resurrection

death   gift   cleanse   rebirth   holy   initiation

sin   reborn   church   grace   oil   godparents

promise   renounce   savior   witness   joy   forgiveness

love   baptism   sanctify   wonder

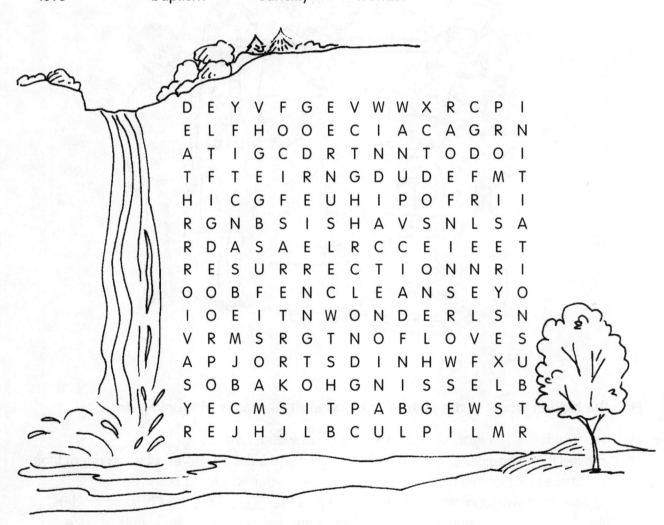

D E Y V F G E V W W X R C P I
E L F H O O E C I A C A G R N
A T I G C D R T N N T O D O I
T F T E I R N G D U D E F M T
H I C G F E U H I P O F R I I
R G N B S I S H A V S N L S A
R D A S A E L R C C E I E E T
R E S U R R E C T I O N N R I
O O B F E N C L E A N S E Y O
I O E I T N W O N D E R L S N
V R M S R G T N O F L O V E S
A P J O R T S D I N H W F X U
S O B A K O H G N I S S E L B
Y E C M S I T P A B G E W S T
R E J H J L B C U L P I L M R

Water Facts

Follow each stream to its pool to discover some important water facts.

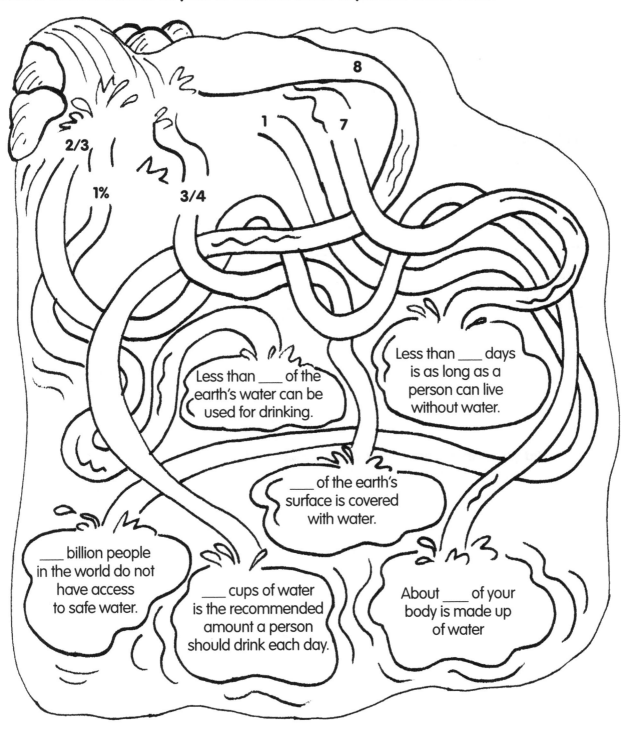

2/3

1%

3/4

8

1

7

Less than ___ of the earth's water can be used for drinking.

Less than ___ days is as long as a person can live without water.

___ of the earth's surface is covered with water.

___ billion people in the world do not have access to safe water.

___ cups of water is the recommended amount a person should drink each day.

About ___ of your body is made up of water

My Daily Water Use

Devote one day to measuring your water use. Mark each time you:

flush a toilet ✔ _____

wash hands or face _____

take a bath or shower _____

use the dishwasher _____

drink water _____

use a washing machine _____

brush teeth _____

water plants _____

rinse or wash dishes in a sink _____

(other uses) _____

_____

_____

What did you notice about your daily water use?

Baptismal Ministry

After his baptism, Jesus was driven into the wilderness where he was tested by Satan. Jesus turned away from the devil's temptations by remembering and asserting who he is: God's beloved son. He returned from the wilderness to begin his public ministry of teaching, healing, and loving.

When we come to the baptismal waters, we renounce Satan and evil. To renounce means to say "no" to something. Then we say, "Yes!" to Jesus and God's love.

Once we are baptized, we also have a public ministry. We are called to use the gifts God has given us to carry on Christ's work in the world, to love God, and to love our neighbor. We make promises to make the world a better place. And we ask for God's help to keep these promises.

Continuing to Grow in Faith

Through our baptism we promise: to continue to learn about all that Jesus taught, to follow the good examples of Christians who have gone before us, to be fed at God's table, and to pray.

Match these people of faith to their words and work about water.

Archbishop Desmond Tutu, b.1931

St. Christopher, 3rd century

Martin Luther King, Jr., 1929-1968

Mother Teresa, 1910-1997

St. Margaret of Scotland, 1045-1093

Washed the feet of the poor as Christ washed the feet of the disciples.

Wrote, "Water is precious; it is the very source of life and a free gift from the Creator. It comes in the morning dew, the soft drizzle and the drumming of heavy drops running into water pipes....How very differently we would regard water if we had to carry every drop we used ourselves."

Gave a speech saying, "we are determined… to work and fight until 'justice runs down like water, and righteousness like a mighty stream.'" Amos 5:24

Chose to serve Christ by assisting people to ford a dangerous river. Once found himself carrying Christ as a child on his shoulders.

Once said, "We ourselves feel that what we are doing is just a drop in the ocean. But the ocean would be less because of that missing drop."

Resisting Evil

Through our baptism we promise: to resist evil, and when we do fall into sin, we promise to turn back to God. None of us is perfect. We spend our entire lives learning to be the people God created us to be. When we hurt others along the way, we need to say we are sorry and ask for their forgiveness and God's.

A Prayer of Forgiveness

For the times I have forgotten that water is a gift,
Forgive me God.

For the times I have ignored the water needs of others,
Forgive me God.

For the times I have been unthinking in my water use,
Forgive me God.

For the times my life choices have polluted water that others need,
Forgive me God.

For _____
Forgive me God.

With your loving help, O God, may I continue to resist the evil forces in this world that cause so many of my sisters and brothers to go thirsty and may I learn more and more how to share the abundance that I have. Amen.

Bearing the Good News

Through our baptism we promise: to share God's Good News in what we do and say. The new life in Christ that baptism brings us is indeed good news for all who are lost or hurting. As people who have received the gift of new life in Baptism, we are called to share that gift with others.

How are these people sharing good news? Write a caption for each picture.

Loving our Neighbors

Through our baptism we promise: to love our <u>neighbors</u> as ourselves. One way to love our neighbors is to share water. When we are responsible about our <u>water</u> use, there can be enough <u>safe</u> and clean water for everyone. When our neighbors have the water they need, they can <u>share</u> it with us. God's <u>love</u> always comes full circle.

When we have enough water, we can _____ it with our neighbors.

We are baptized with _____ that has been in the world since creation.

We spread God's _____ when we work together so everyone can have access to clean and safe water.

Our baptism calls us to go out into the world and seek _____ to serve.

Use the underlined words to complete this water journey.

Striving for Justice

Through our baptism we promise: to work for justice for all people and to respect the dignity of every human being.

Almost one billion people do not have access to clean water. That is one in eight people. Many people must walk long distances from their homes to get water. Then they have to carry the water home. Children who have to spend time everyday carrying water have little time for school or play. Sometimes this water comes from water holes or rivers that are not even clean. Polluted water can cause illness in families.

What can you do?

When we work with others to build wells, latrines, and water stations to provide access to water resources and prevent water-borne illnesses, we are striving for justice and treating others with dignity.

There are many organizations working to provide people across the globe with sustainable access to safe drinking water and basic sanitation. Discuss with your household, church or school how you might work to bring water justice to others. See the resources on p. 48 for some ideas.

Following Jesus

Our baptismal promises compel us to see Christ in the persons we serve. How can we serve Christ in others?

Decode this scripture passage to discover the opportunities.
- cross out the following letters: b, j, q, x and z.
- copy the remaining letters in order into the spaces provided to reveal this important scripture passage.

_____

_____

_____

_____

_____. (Matthew 25:35-36)

Jesus' Water Ministry

Complete each sentence to solve this crossword. For extra clues, look up the verses.*

Across

3. Jesus told Simon to put out into deep water and let down the nets for a _____. (Luke 5:1-11)

4. Jesus invites all who are _____ to come to him. (John 7:37-39)

6. The Samaritan woman who met Jesus at the well asked him, "Where do you get that _____ water?" (John 4:10-11)

8. In the city of Cana, Jesus turned water into wine at a _____. (John 2:1-11)

9. While Jesus slept on the boat, his disciples became afraid because of a fierce _____. (Matthew 8:23-27)

Down

1. The disciples were afraid when they saw Jesus _____ on the sea. (Matthew 14:22-27)

2. Jesus was _____ in the river Jordan. (Mark 1:9-11)

5. In the story Jesus tells, the wise man who builds his house on the rock is safe from the _____. (Matthew 7:24-27)

7. To show his love for them, Jesus washed the disciples' _____. (John 13:1-5)

*For best results, use the NRSV translation of the bible.

How Much Water

does it take...

To bathe?

Take a bath filling the tub to the usual amount you like. Note how full the tub is. Next time you shower, plug the drain. Take your normal length shower. How much does the tub fill? When do you use more water, taking a shower or taking a bath?

To brush your teeth?

Plug the sink drain when you brush your teeth. How much does the sink fill? Next time try filling a cup with water first, and then use that water to brush your teeth. How much water does this save?

To wash your hands?

Plug the sink drain when you wash your hands. How much does the sink fill? You can conserve water when you wash your hands by wetting you hands first, turning off the water while you soap you hands, and then rinsing your hands quickly.

To use the kitchen sink?

Plug the drain in your kitchen sink for a day. How often do you use the sink to rinse or wash or get water? How much does the sink fill in a day? You can conserve when you wash dishes by filling a dish tub with soapy water to wash the dishes, putting the soapy dishes in a dish rack, and then rinsing them. Leaving them in the rack to air dry also conserves energy.

How else can you conserve water?

Living Water

Jesus, tired from a journey, sat down by a well. A Samaritan woman came to draw water from the well and Jesus offers her living water. The woman replies, "Sir, you have no bucket and the well is deep. Where do you get that living water?" (John 4:6-15)

What would living water be? Jesus offers water that assuages more than everyday thirst.

When we choose to pay attention to our own water use and to work for all people to have enough water, we can help those who thirst daily. When we reach out in true kindness to others, it is like giving them buckets that they can fill with life-giving water.

Search for these drops of living water in the well.

kindness	peace	integrity	empathy	compassion
humility	justice	respect	reverence	gentleness
delight	dignity	generosity	hospitality	truthfulness
joy	love	care	service	understanding

```
E C I V R E S C Y H E J P Z Q O E G U Y
F U P P O D T S O T U C O K C E M E E J
K I N D N E S S T M I M A Y O V P N C T
E C I T S U J H B T P R I E U O A T N C
I B G F R J G M J Q H A G L P L T L E E
M H O S P I T A L I T Y S E I V H E R P
S S E N L U F H T U R T N S T T Y N E S
U N D E R S T A N D I N G K I N Y E V E
X C D I G N I T Y C A R E S E O I S E R
Y T I S O R E N E G W S T Q X N N S R Y
```

Thirsting for God

As a deer longs for flowing streams, so longs my soul for you, O God. (Psalm 42:1)

Find a path for the deer to reach the stream.

Thirst

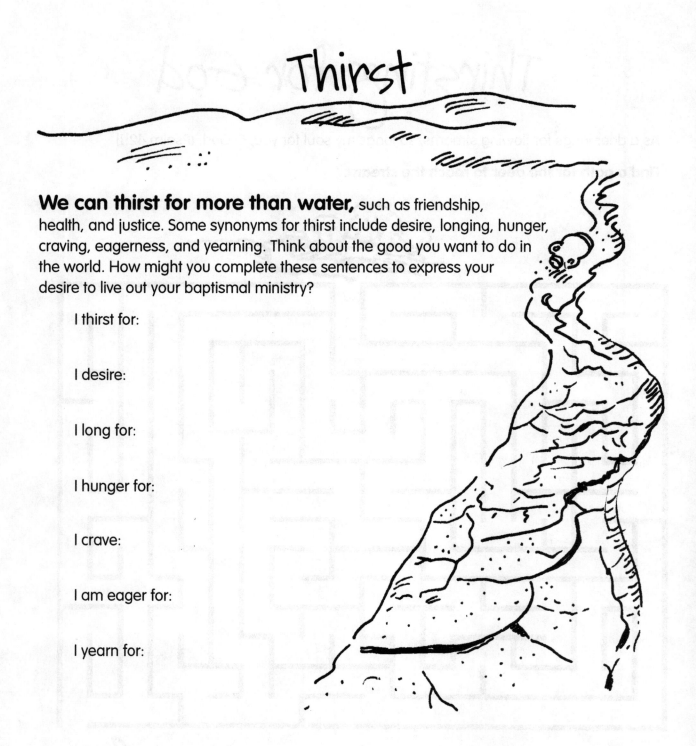

We can thirst for more than water, such as friendship, health, and justice. Some synonyms for thirst include desire, longing, hunger, craving, eagerness, and yearning. Think about the good you want to do in the world. How might you complete these sentences to express your desire to live out your baptismal ministry?

I thirst for:

I desire:

I long for:

I hunger for:

I crave:

I am eager for:

I yearn for:

Jesus said, "Blessed are those who hunger and thirst for righteousness, for they will be filled."
(Matthew 5:6)

The Gift of Water

An Outdoor Prayer Walk

- Choose a place to begin your walk. This can be your neighborhood, a park, a forest, a desert, or a city street.

- Begin by standing still. Take three slow, deep breaths. Imagine the water available in this place. What do you think you will discover on your walk? Do you feel drawn to begin your walk in a particular direction?

- As you begin your walk, imagine that Jesus goes before you. Notice any water around you. It there moisture in the air? In your body? Are you thirsty?

- Notice any water in this environment. Is it naturally occurring (like a stream or dew on the grass) or has it been provided by humans (like a fire hydrant or a canal that has been dug)? Give thanks for this water.

- Pay attention to your senses as you encounter water in this environment. What does the water look like? Smell like? Feel like? Taste like? Sound like?

- Imagine all the animals and people who enjoy or depend on this water. Give thanks for all the creatures. Give thanks for the people. Pray that they may respect this natural resource and use it wisely.

- As you continue your walk, pay attention to your thoughts. Does anything surprise you as you consider the water in this place? Did you discover more or less water in this particular environment than you imagined?

- As you complete your walk, offer gratitude for all that you have encountered. Give thanks for the water cycle. Give thanks for the waters of baptism. Give thanks for God's love, which always comes full circle.

The Gift of Water

An Indoor Prayer Walk

◊ Choose a place to begin your walk. This can be your home, school, or church.

◊ Begin by standing still in the entrance. Take three slow, deep breaths. Imagine the water being used in this place. What do you think you will discover on your walk?

◊ As you begin your walk, imagine that Jesus goes before you. Notice any water around you. Is there moisture in the air? In your body? Are you thirsty?

◊ Visit each room and notice how water is present. Think of all the ways water is used in that room. Give thanks for that water.

◊ Think of the people who use the water in each room. Pray that they may use the water wisely. Give thanks for these people.

◊ As you walk from room to room, pay attention to your thoughts. Does anything surprise you as you consider the water in this place? Did you discover more or less water being used than you imagined?

◊ As you finish your walk, return to the place where you began. Give thanks for the water cycle. Give thanks for the waters of baptism. Give thanks for God's love, which always comes full circle.

Harvesting Rainwater

To harvest means to gather. Did you know you could harvest rainwater? This ancient technique is now being used across the globe to maintain good water stewardship.

Find and name these places around the world where rainwater harvesting is being used successfully to provide water for drinking, watering livestock and irrigate gardens.

Uganda   Brazil   China   Bermuda   Texas (in the United States)

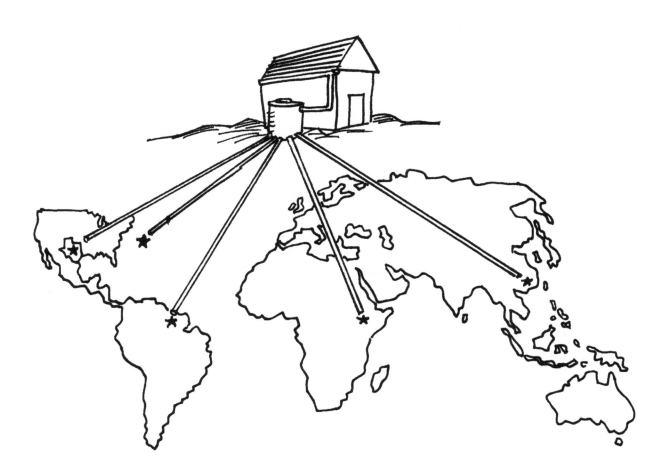

Safe in a Storm

Jonah was caught in a storm at sea:

Such a mighty storm came upon the sea that the ship threatened to break up. (Jonah 1:4)
God saved the people on board and spared Jonah.

The disciples were caught in a storm at sea:

A great windstorm arose, and the waves beat into the boat, so that the boat was already being swamped. (Mark 4:37)
Jesus spoke to the wind and stilled the storm.

St. Paul was caught in a storm at sea:

When neither the sun nor stars appeared for many days, and no small tempest raged, all hope of our being saved was at last abandoned. Acts 27:20
Paul continued to trust in God and all on board reached shore safely.

Jonah, the disciples and St. Paul all found themselves safe on the other side of the storm and knew that God had delivered them.

When have you found yourself in a storm? How is God with you in the stormy times of your life? Many people pray during tumultuous times. What would you pray? Write or draw about this.

> Calm me, Lord, as you stilled the storm.
> Still me Lord and keep me from harm.
> Let all the tumult within me cease.
> Enfold me, Lord, in your peace.
> > *Celtic Prayer*

> Dear God, be good to me;
> The sea is so wide and my boat is so small.
> > *Breton Fisherman's Prayer*

Sharing Abundance

Find a small container you can recycle, like a coffee tin or an oatmeal box. Decorate it with water images. Use it to collect coins.

Each day for a week drop into your collection bottle:

- a penny each time you get ice

- a nickel each time you take a drink of water

- a dime each time you wash your hands or face

- a quarter each time you water a plant

- a quarter each time you fill your pet's water bowl

- two quarters each time you run the dishwasher

- a dollar each time you do a load of laundry

- (add your own idea)_____

_____

_____

Donate the money you collect to an organization that works to provide safe water. See the resources on p. 48 for ideas.

Try this:
Keep up your collection for a month.
Encourage each member of your household to contribute.
Invite your friends at church or school to collect coins with you.

Remember Your Baptism

To actively remember something means to recall it, consider it, and be mindful of it. How might you remember your baptism in the week ahead?

💧 ask a parent or godparent to tell you the story of your baptism

💧 plan a party to celebrate your baptismal anniversary

💧 take a shower; as the water pours over you imagine it washing away your sins and bringing you new life

💧 go for a walk in the rain and splash in puddles to celebrate the gift of water

💧 place a bowl of water by your bed; before you go to bed at night and when you wake up in the morning touch the water and thank God for your baptism

💧 write a letter to a godparent and share how you are living your life

💧 paint your idea of baptism using water colors

💧 create a slide show of images that remind you of baptism

A Cloud of Witnesses

We believe that one day God's creation will be perfected. Then, "They will hunger no more, and thirst no more; the sun will not strike them, nor any scorching heat; for the Lamb at the center of the throne will be their shepherd, and he will guide them to springs of the water of life, and God will wipe away every tear from their eyes." (Revelation 7:15-17)

Connect the dots to discover the source of perfect life.

Holy Water

"How I use water or fuel is intimately connected to the ability of people across the globe to live."

Katherine Jefferts Schori
Presiding Bishop of the Episcopal Church
Sermon at Episcopal Youth Event – June 23, 2011

All water is recycled water. Water is not made new, but moves through God's creation across time and oceans. The water we bless in baptism is the same water through which the ark carried the animals safely through the flood. It is the same water through which the Israelites crossed into the Promised Land. It is the same water that John used to baptize Jesus in the Jordan. It is the same water that was poured over you in baptism.

All water is holy water. Respect it. Honor it. Receive it as a gift.
Share it abundantly with others. Drink deeply and joyfully.

Answer Key

The Water Cycle (p. 10) Words counter-clockwise: condensation, precipitation, infiltration, percolation, transpiration, evaporation

Crossing the Red Sea (p. 14) chase, extremely, could, clogged, returned, waters = Exodus

Water Images (p. 15) Across: 5. waves 6. torrents 8. rain 10. clouds 11. springs 13. streams
Down: 1. dew 2. river 3. fountain 4. water 6. thirsts 7. pools 9. tears 12. seas

John the Baptist (p. 19) creation, obey, prepared, people, countryside, baptize = repent

Blessing the Water (p. 21) In order: gift, Holy Spirit, promise, baptism, Messiah, death, sin, water, Christ, reborn

Searching the Waters (p. 22)

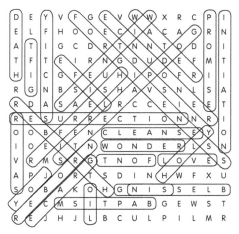

Water Facts (p. 23) ¾ of the earth's surface is covered with water. About ⅔ of your body is made up of water. 1 billion people in the world to not have access to safe water. 8 cups of water is the recommended amount a person should drink each day. Less than 1% of the earth's water can be used for drinking. Less than 7 days is as long as a person can live without water.

Continuing to Grow in Faith (p. 26) Desmond Tutu wrote, "Water is precious; . ."; St. Christopher chose to serve Christ by assisting people to ford a dangerous river; St. Margaret: Washed the feet of the poor; Martin Luther King, Jr., gave a speech saying, "we are determined . . ."; Mother Teresa once said, "We ourselves feel that what we are doing is just a drop . . ."

Loving our Neighbors (p. 29) When we have enough water, we can share it with our neighbors. We spread God's love when we work together so everyone can have access to clean and safe water. Our baptism calls us to go out into the world and seek neighbors to serve. We are baptized with water that has been in the world since creation.

Following Jesus (p. 31) For I was hungry and you gave me food, I was thirsty and you gave me something to drink, I was a stranger and you welcomed me, I was naked and you gave me clothing, I was sick and you took care of me, I was in prison and you visited me.

Jesus' Water Ministry (p. 32) Across: 3. catch 4. thirsty 6. living 8. wedding 9. storm Down: 1. walking 2. baptized 5. floods 7. feet

Living Water (p. 33)

```
E C I V R E S C Y H E J P Z Q O E G U Y
F U P P O D T S O T U C O K C E M E E J
K I N D N E S S T M I M A Y O V P N C T
E C I T S U J H B T P R I E U O A N E C
I B G F R J G M J Q H A G L P L T H N E
M H O S P I T A L I T Y S E I V H E R P
S S E N L U F H T U R T N S T T Y R E S
U N D E R S T A N D I N G K I N Y E V E
X C D I G N I T Y C A R E S E O I S E R
Y T I S O R E N E G W S T Q X N N S R Y
```

Harvesting Rainwater (p. 39)

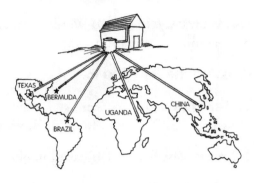

A Cloud of Witnesses (p. 43) The Lamb of God – Agnus Dei

Glossary

Baptism: the sacrament of Christian initiation. Through baptism, God adopts us as God's children and makes us members of the Body of Christ. The outward and visible sign of baptism is water. The inward and spiritual grace of baptism includes forgiveness of sin and new life in the Holy Spirit. People are baptized in the Name of the Father, and of the Son and of the Holy Spirit. For further information, see pp. 298 and 858 in The Book of Common Prayer.

The Baptismal Covenant: a confession of faith found in The Book of Common Prayer (1979). It is based on ancient baptismal formulas in which a person had to state (or confess) her or his belief in core Christian doctrines before being baptized. Such baptismal formulas later became our creeds, or statements of belief (such as the Apostles' Creed and the Nicene Creed). The Baptismal Covenant includes five questions that spell out how we are to live a Christian life and keep God's commandments. As a whole, it defines our relationship with God and offers us a guideline as to how to respond faithfully to God's love for us.

The Book of Common Prayer: the authorized prayer book of The Episcopal Church. It contains the regular rites and ceremonies of worship in The Episcopal Church, including Holy Baptism and Holy Eucharist. It also includes the book of psalms, historical documents, and An Outline of the Faith. It is often referred to as the BCP. Thomas Cranmer wrote the first Book of Common Prayer in 1549 for use in the Church of England. The first American prayer book was compiled in 1789, followed by revisions in 1892, 1928 and 1979. The Episcopal Church also authorizes supplemental texts for worship as the church continues to deepen its understanding of prayer and mission.

Condensation: the process by which water vapor in the atmosphere chills, changing from a gas to a liquid and forming clouds and water droplets.

Covenant: a sacred agreement between God and God's people that expresses a relationship based on love and faithfulness.

Evaporation: the process by which water, warmed by the air, changes from a liquid into a gas becoming water vapor and rising into the atmosphere.

The Exodus: the story of the departure of the Israelites from Egypt where they had been held captive as slaves under Pharaoh.

Infiltration: the process by which water enters the soil or subsurface.

Millennium Development Goals (MDGs): eight international development goals adopted by the United Nations aimed at ending extreme poverty. One of the goals specifically address environmental sustainability and seeks to reduce by half the number of people without access to clean and safe water by 2015.

Percolation: the movement of water through the soil and its layers, by gravity.

Precipitation: water that falls to the earth as rain, snow, sleet, hail or other near-liquid forms.

Rainwater Harvesting: accumulating and storing rainwater for use in households and gardens. Rainwater collected from roofs can be used for drinking water, irrigating crops and watering livestock.

Recycle: to convert used materials into new products, or reuse materials and substances rather than discard them. To prevent waste.

Sacraments: the "outward and visible signs of inward and spiritual grace" given to us by Christ to ensure we receive that grace. The two great sacraments of the church are Holy Baptism and Holy Eucharist. For further information, see The Book of Common Prayer, p. 857-858

Stewardship: the responsibility to take care of something that belongs to someone else. The endeavor to manage resources reliably and effectively. The care of God's creation.

Sustainability: the endurance of natural resources in order to support life. The capability to conserve and maintain natural resources so as not to deplete them.

Transpiration: the process by which plants release water vapor into the atmosphere.

The Water Cycle: a model of the continuous movement of water from the surface of the Earth into the atmosphere and back through the processes of evaporation, transpiration, condensation, precipitation and infiltration. Also known as the hydraulic cycle.

Resources

Books

Kitch, Anne E. *Taking the Plunge: Baptism and Parenting.* New York: Morehouse Publishing, 2006.

Nunley, Jan, Claire Foster & David Shreeve. *How Many Lightbulbs Does it Take to Change a Christian: A Pocket Guide to Shrinking Your Ecological Footprint.* New York: Church Publishing, 2008.

Marks, William E., editor. *Water Voices from Around the World* .Water Voices, Inc., 2007.

Pritchard, Gretchen Wolff. *New Life: The Sunday Paper's Baptism Book.* New Haven, CT: The Sunday Paper, 1986.

Tammany, Klara. *Living Water: Baptism as a Way of Life.* New York: Church Publishing, 2002.

Organizations

Bill & Melinda Gates Foundation • *www.gatesfoundation.org*
- supports sanitation initiatives including Reinventing the Toilet

Episcopal Relief and Development (ERD) • *www.er-d.org*
- worldwide relief agency of the Episcopal Church
- website provides educational resources such as Abundant Garden Project, Act Out Clean Water Project and the Gifts for Life catalogue

Living Water International • *www.water.cc*
- implements community-based water solutions in developing countries
- website provides educational resources and opportunities to donate

Millennium Development Goals • *www.un.org/millenniumgoals/*
- initiative of the United Nations to end extreme poverty in the world

National Oceanic and Atmospheric Administration • *www.education.noaa.gov*
- educational resource for water issues

UN Water • *www.unwater.org*
- strengthens coordination and coherence among UN entities dealing with issues related to all aspects of freshwater and sanitation
- website provides activities related to World Water Day

The U.S. Geological Survey • *www.water.usgs.gov*
- educational resource for water issues

Water Supply and Sanitation Collaborative Council • *www.wsscc.org*
- website provides information on rainwater harvesting

World Water Council • *www.worldwatercouncil.org*
- brings together organizations to facilitate water sustainability.